My Journey with the Qur'an

With Useful Advice on Memorization

Souad Brown Mhani

Strategic Book Publishing and Rights Co.

Strategic Book Publishing and Rights Co., LLC
USA | Singapore
www.sbpra.net

For information about special discounts for bulk purchases, please contact Strategic Book Publishing and Rights Co. Special Sales, at bookorder@sbpra.net.

ISBN: 978-1-68235-310-3

Book Design: Suzanne Kelly

DEDICATION

*I dedicate this book to my father
who led by an exceptional example.*

To my beloved mother.

*To my loving husband who managed
to be nothing but supportive of my objectives
in writing this book.*

*And to my great children, Nisreen, Malak,
Nouhaila, Mohammed-Waleed.*

To my Brothers and Sisters

"There certainly has come to you from Allah a light and a clear Book through which Allah guides those who seek His pleasure to the ways of peace, brings them out of darkness and into light by His Will, and guides them to the Straight Path."[5:15-16].

This is a promise from Allah (SWT)...

CHAPTER ONE

A ll Muslims aspire to memorize some of the Qur'an.
Many are blessed with the ability to memorize more
easily than others. In fact, some memorize the entire
Qur'an, *Alhamdulillah*. This book is about my journey
through the steps I took to complete my memorization of
the Qur'an. It is a journey that I hope you find fascinating and inspiring, one that leads you, or maybe a family
member, to join the next generation of *hafidh* or *hafidha*
(a person who has memorized the whole Qur'an) carrying
the Qur'an in their heart rather than on paper or computer
disks, as it is Allah (SWT) who has promised to protect
and preserve His book.

Remember the famous saying of Imam Malik in his
Muwatta (may Allah be pleased with him), the leading
scholar in Madinah during the *tabi'een* and *tabi' tabi'een*
(the children and the grandchildren of the *Sahabah
(companions of the Prophet)*). When you are asked by
some Muslims of today who may not understand because
their knowledge of *Kitab wa Sunnah* (the Holy Book and
the example set by the Prophet) is deficient and they ask
you: Why do you spend all of this time to memorize the

Qur'an when today we have what they did not have in the time of Rasullullah (the Messenger of Allah) (PBUH)— recording devices, the whole Qur'an on tape and on computer disk, recited by the best of the best reciters of the last hundred years, like Shaykh Abdul Basset Abdusamad of Egypt, Shaykh Bin Baz of Saudi Arabia, and the one I am currently listening to, Mahmoud Khalil Al Husary, and others? Therefore, you and we do not need to spend all of this time memorizing.

Imam Malik was asked something to the effect of: Why do you spend so much time memorizing the Qur'an and all these *hadith (a testimony of what the Prophet said)* when you already have everything written down in the books you possess?

Imam Malik replied something like, "A man who has not memorized what is in the books *he* possesses could suffer someone changing his books while he sleeps, and he would not know it."

So, I say to my readers: Remember that Allah (SWT) has promised to protect and preserve His Holy Book: "It is certainly We Who have revealed the reminder, and it is certainly We Who will preserve it." (Qur'an 15:9) If electricity is lost, if all computers and electronic devices are destroyed in an international cyberwar between nations, the safest place for the Qur'an is where it has always been since the beginning, in the hearts and minds of mankind.

Those who have memorized the entire Qur'an from the time it was revealed until now, as well as those who do so in the future, are in the special category of mankind that Allah (SWT) has chosen to hold His Qur'an. Allah (SWT) said in His holy book: "Then we caused to inherit the Book those We have chosen of Our servants." (Qur'an 35:32)

My journey with the Qur'an began early in life. I was born and grew up in a nice part of northern Morocco in the town of Aknoul, where a high percentage of the population is devoutly religious. It is also conducive to reflecting and studying because the environment is close to nature, set in the mountains with a basic agricultural lifestyle. That is in contrast to a person growing up in a Fifth Avenue high-rise in New York City. Most Moroccans know that famous musicians like John Lennon, in 1967, and Jimi Hendrix, in 1969, used Essaouira, a city on the coast of northern Morocco, as a retreat to write their music, and many French artists created several of their works there. I was blessed to grow up in such a natural environment like Aknoul's.

Reflecting on my early years, I understand now as a mother why I had the perception that my older sister was the recipient of a better early education. Mothers tend to want the world for their firstborn, trying to give them everything imaginable. Whereas with the second and subsequent children, we tend to adjust our aspirations and desires to something less. The exciting thing is that whilst

I felt deprived when looking at my oldest sister, Hafida, I now realize that the choice made for both of us reflected our natural aptitudes and personalities.

I was kind of envious that my sister learned French at the nursery, but today I cannot imagine myself as a French teacher rather than a teacher of the Qur'an. I am sure back then that my sister could not have imagined she would become a French teacher either. I recall being impressed as I went with my mother to deliver my sister to her nursery. It was such a lively place, modern with all the attractions a child would want. I couldn't wait until my turn came to attend. But the shock for me was that my father had decided that I should attend a *masjid's* (school) *madrassah* instead of a nursery where the kids learn both Arabic and French.

I remember listening to my mother and my father discussing my father's decision, and I was so upset, especially because the madrassah at the masjid (mosque) was no comparison to the amenities at my sister's nursery, which had nice chairs, solid tables, and bright, colorful playthings. At the madrassah, there was not even a chair, except for the imam's. All of the children had to sit on a handmade straw carpet on the floor, no matter how uncomfortable it felt. I remember my legs hurting from crossing them the entire time I was learning. However, after a year there, I began to enjoy the experience. I recall the imam informing my father that I had a natural aptitude for memorizing, and I used to recite the Qur'an aloud at home to practice before the next day's class.

In later years, my experience at the madrassah benefited me when I started my academic study at primary school. I recall being able to remember the lessons more quickly and in more detail than many of my classmates, enabling me to do very well on exams. At the end of the year, I received prizes for my outstanding performance in primary school.

CHAPTER TWO

When I became of age to attend high school, my parents decided to move to the large city of Fez, I presume to take advantage of what large cities offer.

The University of Al Qarawiyyen in the City of Fez is recognized by the Guinness World Records and UNESCO as the oldest existing higher educational institution in the world founded by a Muslim woman named Fatima Al-Fihri in Morocco.

I recall my first day at the high school there, named Lycée Moulay Rachid, feeling a bit out of place because the language in northern Morocco is a bit different from the dialect in central Morocco. It took me a while to adjust to a new school and the new environment, but I soon found myself back in a routine that involved learning the Qur'an. It so happened that on the weekends my friends invited me to come along with them to their Sunday Qur'an classes offered by a university professor who taught Islamic education at his university and was offering weekend Qur'an classes in his spare time. I found the classes easy to absorb, and I made rapid progress.

A short time later I recall going with my mother to visit some relatives, and I recognized two of them as students in the Sunday Qur'an classes, which encouraged me to want to attend the classes even more, now that I knew some of my relatives were going as well. The teacher was strict and used to sit behind a curtain so that he would not directly look at the ladies and girls, and he would have his daughter collect our written questions from the other side of the curtain.

This learning experience with the Qur'an continued through to my years at Sidi Mohamed Ben Abdellah University, Faculty of Letters and Human Sciences Dhar Mahraz-Fez, but in a private class outside the university with several different Qur'an and *Tajweed* (the set of rules under which the words in the Qur'an should be pronounced during its recitation) teachers.

The funny thing is that my sister and I were at the university at the same time, but she chose to specialize in Islamic studies, and I chose the nonreligious subject of English Literature, almost the opposite experience of our foundation years. The reason for this was because my sister felt that Islamic studies was easier, and she tried to convince me to take it as well, but I had decided that I wanted a change from Qur'an and Islamic studies, so I ended up choosing English Literature, as the destiny of Allah (SWT) would have it. Today, my sister is a French language teacher, and I have been blessed with the opportunity to share my knowledge in memorization of the Qur'an and the Tajweed rules with others.

This is just background, not my introduction to learning the Qur'an, but now I will begin to teach you what I have learned through my journey.

CHAPTER THREE

A year after I graduated from university with a bachelor's degree in English Literature, I lived in different parts of the world including Bermuda, a small, beautiful island that reminded me of Aknoul, the town where I lived my childhood. I was in the middle of the Atlantic Ocean off the coast of North Carolina in America. Bermuda was close to nature and didn't have the distractions of a big city. There were nice beaches with pink sand, lots of parks and golf courses, boating, swimming, fishing, and lots of green space. I call it paradise on earth.

My husband's friend, Sheikh Elalami , a Moroccan imam (imam is a Muslim pastor) , was one of the senior imams at Masjid Muhammad, the local masjid (mosque), and was an expert teacher of all aspects of Qur'an and himself a hafidh.

I became friends with two Moroccan ladies, and we decided to use our free time constructively by learning more about the Qur'an. The three of us ended up attending Sheikh Alamie's Qur'an classes for a short time, where I elected to learn *Riwayat Hafs 'an 'Asim* recitation style, since I was already familiar with *Riwayat Warsh 'an Naafi*. Embarking on learning the two different sets of Tajweed rules rekindled my interest to memorize the Qur'an, and though I had decided to concentrate on memorization, my intention at that moment was also to focus on Tajweed rules.

A short time later, the Moroccan imam had to return to his country because he wanted his children to grow up in his home country and to learn the Qur'an there. When we met him in 2019, several decades after he had left Bermuda, we found out that one of his sons has also become a hafidh *ma Sha Allah*.

Later on, another imam from Morocco was hired by the local Bermuda masjid (mosque) to teach at their Islamic school when Sheikh Elalami left. However, that other imam, after spending some years in Bermuda, had to also return to Morocco, and I was asked to replace him on a temporary basis until they found a replacement teacher. I saw this as an opportunity to gain further experience, and therefore gave my affirmative response.

Years earlier in Morocco I had obtained teaching experience as a volunteer at Centre Ahli, a center for homeless children. I used to go there twice a week, and the children were always eager to learn the English language that I taught them. I also taught them life skills, and at the same time the children taught me how to teach special education needs (SEN), as some of them were challenged students with behavioral problems. This experience provided me with skills that helped me in my teaching profession. It was the first teaching job I had, and I wish I could meet the now-grown adults someday to see how they developed. My experience at the center during the free time I had from my university classes helped me to become confident as a teacher since I now knew I had a special aptitude for it.

So, I ended up teaching at the CMS (Clara Muhammad School) for three years as a part-time teacher, which confirmed my earlier decision, because those three years gave me a strong foundation in teaching generally and teaching the Qur'an specifically. I was driven to become an exceptional teacher of the Qur'an because I felt any future student of mine deserved above-average instruction.

"This is Aidan in my classroom at Clara Mohammed School in 2016."
I encourage parents to teach Qur'an to their children at a young age.
Do not wait to the summer school break but fit it in during the school
year to the extent the children can manage. Always reward and praise
them after each achievement, as children do not understand what they
cannot see but rather physical benefits. Teach your children Qur'an,
and Qur'an will teach them everything.

I was learning Tajweed rules online with some good teachers. I take this opportunity to thank those teachers, especially teacher Salwa and others, as they were of great help to me in my journey with the Qur'an. I would also like to thank the headteacher at the local masjid's (mosque's) madrassa, the Clara Muhammad School, for giving me the opportunity to gain even more teaching experience. May Allah (SWT) continue to shower them with His blessings and reward them immensely.

CHAPTER FOUR

On your journey with the Qur'an, trust me, you will find the natural distractions of everyday life to be challenging, but you have to remain determined and focused to reach your goal. Let me share with you some of the challenges at the beginning of my journey and how I promised myself to complete the Qur'an, no matter what obstacles I encountered.

In November 2013, my cousin—may Allah (SWT) have mercy on her—who was like a sister to me and almost the same age as me, passed away at a young age, approximately six months after she gave birth to her only child, a son. It was at this time that I realized that death could come at any age, therefore we have to be prepared, so I started to devote even more time to my religious observances. I found that immersing myself in the recitation of the Qur'an was comforting. I decided to continue with the Qur'an from that point with more conviction and to its conclusion.

I began my noble quest by searching for online Qur'an classes and registering with the best teachers. I started with Qur'an recitation at surah (chapter) Al-Baqarah, observing strict Tajweed rules but more deeply under the critical analysis of my teacher. Starting with surah Al-Baqarah reminded me of growing up when my mother used to turn on the recording of that surah in the mornings to help us wake up in the right frame of mind. This early experience also helped me to move through the beginning part of the surah quickly, as it was so familiar.

Toward completing my memorization of surah Al-Baqarah, my challenges and tests from Allah (SWT) began. We know that the prophets (PBUT) were tested, and I was determined to persevere the way they had. For example, let's look at the prophet Ayyub (AS) (named Job in the Bible), who was also tested: "Indeed, We found him patient, an excellent servant. Indeed, he was one repeatedly turning back [to Allah]." (Qur'an 38:44) Many scholars considered that his example teaches us to remain patient no matter what we experience. "There was certainly in their stories a lesson for those of understanding." (Qur'an 12:111)

This was driven home to me by some of my close Uyghur friends who were married to husbands who were also Uyghur and who spent many years in the US military prison in Guantanamo Bay, Cuba, and were released after they were proven innocent of what they had been accused of. They told me that their husbands used to recite this *ayah (verse)*:

And surely we try you with something of fear and hunger, and loss of wealth and crops, but give glad tidings to the steadfast, who when a misfortune befalls them, say lo! we are Allah's (possession of Allah) and to Him shall we surely return. Such are they on whom are blessings from their Lord, and mercy. Such are the rightly-guided. (Qur'an 2:155-157)

My friend explained that it took her husband two years to memorize the Qur'an while he was an innocent person in jail, and that overall about four hundred prisoners did the same thing during that time. She explained to me that having memorized the whole Qur'an, her husband became refocused on making a good life for himself and his family, and a state of peacefulness and happiness took over his personality. For me, and for anyone who memorizes the entire Qur'an, you gain a perspective of life that reflects the message of the Qur'an rather than of materialism. A person becomes enthused to share the knowledge of the Qur'an because you want others to experience the same benefit.

This new country I had moved to, Bermuda, although a small island, had made a courageous decision to help President Barak Obama close the US military prison in Cuba. Bermuda had sent a private jet to Cuba to pick up the four Uyghur men after all the other Uyghurs at the prison had been proven to be innocent, and Bermuda agreed to give them a home for humanitarian reasons. My friends later traveled from their respective Uyghur communities to Bermuda to marry these men, all of whom were proficient in the recitation of the Qur'an, and two of them are hafidhs.

In my own situation of personal trials, I recall I used to repeat the following *dua (invocation an act of supplication)* a lot: "O Allah, reward me for my affliction and give me something better than it in exchange for it." After I lost my cousin, I believe Allah (SWT) answered my dua, because soon afterward I became pregnant with my son Mohammed-Waleed after having three girls.

However, my pregnancy was problematic, and my doctor was worried I might not carry the pregnancy to full term. I prayed to Allah (SWT), and I kept my faith strong. I also faced the difficult decision of taking an opportunity that presented itself: to perform *Umrah* (the lesser pilgrimage) or stay at home. One of my friends who is a nurse advised me not to travel because she was concerned about the history of my pregnancy. However, something told me to trust in Allah (SWT) and visit His house. The complication of my pregnancy included spotting frequently from day one of pregnancy, and I was concerned that, in addition to the risk of losing the pregnancy, I might not be able to perform the rituals of Umrah. Although we experienced difficulties a year earlier in trying to perform Umrah, I felt reassured we would be successful this time.

The year before, we had encountered delays in receiving our Umrah visas and had to cancel our plans because we no longer had the time to detour to Morocco to leave the three girls with my mother. So, we asked the agent to return our passports. We took our passports from the New York agency and gave them to another agency, this time in Morocco, in the hope that they could process the visa more quickly. However, this was not to be, and we cancelled our plans. I was terribly upset, as I thought that I might be one of those that Allah (SWT) may not choose to visit His house. However, on this occasion I believed everything would go smoothly.

Also, after we received our visas, the MERS virus emerged in Saudi Arabia, possibly originating from camels, and the authorities decided to stop giving Umrah visas to pregnant ladies and elderly persons. My mother was also concerned about the virus and tried to convince me not to travel, but I already had my visa and took this as a sign of Allah's (SWT) invitation to His house. My beloved husband encouraged me to consider what Allah (SWT) might want to show me by giving me His invitation during these circumstances. I decided to accept Allah's (SWT) invitation, and I also decided to do salat *istikharah* (the prayer of seeking counsel), and it reinforced my decision to perform Umrah.

I decided to visit my gynecologist a few days before I traveled, and she indicated traveling should not present an unusual risk, but she told me to take vitamin-rich drinks to help me regain lost weight. The day before traveling, I waited until evening to pack because I was still uncertain if I should go. The following morning I felt much better, but even though I was leaving my daughters with my sister Loubna, as any mother would appreciate, I had mixed emotions. It was not easy, especially leaving my youngest, beautiful daughter, Nouhaila, who was not quite two years old.

We took the flight to New York's JFK Airport to connect with our Umrah tour group and flew to Jeddah. I was uncomfortable during the thirteen-hour flight, but I managed to sleep a lot. I was excited when we arrived at Jeddah. Then we took a short flight to Madinah just after *maghreb* (sunset), and I remember seeing the lights of Masjid al-Haram for the first time as we were preparing to land. I was so excited and almost forgot all of my worries.

I will never forget that on arriving in Madinah at the impressive Movenpick Hotel I noticed that the persistent spotting stopped, and I did not have that problem throughout my time there.

Five days later, we took a bus to Makkah, and upon arrival at just after 10 p.m., we decided to perform our Umrah immediately that night. I was very tired, but the excitement gave me energy. My only worry was whether or not my spotting would resume before I had the chance to finish. On arrival back to our hotel, I was reassured that my condition was stabilized, and we had successfully completed our Umrah. We spent several days in Makkah, including a visit to Mount Arafat, and returned to Jeddah and back home with no more complications.

This photo was taken in February 2019. Memorization of Qur'an is like doing your walking and running between Safah and Marwa. You can speed up and also slow down but you cannot stop nor not complete the task. Remember the hadith of the Prophet "Allah makes the way to Jannah easy for him who trades the path in search of knowledge" (Muslim).

We took lots of water home from the Zamzam Well to share with our friends, without whose assistance we would not have been able to perform Umrah. I must give special thanks to a large portion of the Muslim community who assisted in caring for our daughters. Also, my pregnancy went fine, and I returned home and gave birth to my much-appreciated son, Mohammed-Waleed, several months later.

Another challenge to my quest of memorization was that within two months of my son being born, we had to move to London in December 2014 for a temporary work assignment for my husband, and I wondered how I would keep to my schedule of memorization. When we arrived to London on the 31st of December and were supposed to go straight to our flat in Bermondsey it was not available so we had to stay in a hotel in central London for approximately one week. When our flat was ready it was cold and only partly furnished with no bedding, imagine my challenge. However, I was well organized and took my tasks in steps. The first thing I organized was the internet connection so that I could do online classes and not miss any lessons. It was during the school term, and I was able to drop my two girls Nisreen and Malak at school, enabling me to focus on my memorization studies throughout each day while they were there.

I quickly discovered the most efficient way for me to memorize was first to write down the ayah I wanted to memorize and translate the words into English to reinforce my broader understanding of how non-Arabic speakers would interpret the ayats. I found this helped with memorization of the Arabic. Another method I used was to write the ayats down on an erasable board, then erase certain words and try to remember what I had erased until I could reach the point of erasing the whole ayah from the board.

Another memorable challenge was when I went to Morocco for a long vacation in 2015. Visiting all the different relatives was a distraction from my study routine, but during Ramadan of that year, I had renewed energy and decided to memorize the whole of surah Al-Baqarah again. In 2013, I had started memorizing surah Al-Baqarah, and when I got near the end I stopped. Therefore, it reassured me when I was able to resume my memorization starting with the same surah.

I informed my teacher of my intentions, and she encouraged me to pursue my objective. I managed to memorize all of surah Al-Baqarah by the end of that Ramadan. This experience encouraged me to accelerate my memorization because, as you all know, surah Al-Baqarah is the longest surah in the Qur'an, and I realized if I could memorize the longest surah quickly, I would certainly be able to memorize the rest of them.

I also recall an interesting experience that strengthened my desire to achieve my goal when I joined my online classes run by Al-Mistabah in 2014. The classes I joined consisted of teachers with the highest credentials from all over the Muslim world. I had a wise, strict teacher who was originally from Egypt, who I found out later was a recipient of an unbroken chain of instructors that went all the way back to the time of the Prophet Muhammad (PBUH). She was also a hafidha and was trained in the ten Qira'at; this encouraged me even further. My study group included two of my beloved cousins, and we encouraged each other, but I knew I was not giving one-hundred-percent effort.

One morning I received a message from my teacher stating that she was transferring me to a lower class, which meant I would be separated from my two cousins. I pleaded with the teacher to keep me in the higher class. She refused and said I needed to prove myself over a period of time, after which she would reconsider. So, I worked hard for the next two or three weeks, sending all my recitation in on time and showing all my enthusiasm. She responded approximately three weeks later and put me back in my original class with my cousins. Now I deeply appreciate her psychology of teaching. I was disappointed when she informed all her students that she was moving and wouldn't be able to teach us any longer.

It has been my experience that teaching the Qur'an also helps to reinforce my memorization at the subconscious level. This is one reason why I accepted the request to teach the children of some of my friends. After a short period of time, the number of children outgrew the space in my house, so I asked the headteacher at CMS (Clara Muhammad School) if I could use one of their classrooms so I could expand the number of children to include children who attended the masjid's madrasah. At approximately the same time, I had volunteered to teach at the masjid school during the week. Therefore, it was decided that I could use the same room at the masjid on weekends for teaching ladies and children.

As for striving to reach any objective, you have to plan your time using a schedule that is realistic for you. Otherwise, you will not be able to adhere to it. In my case, I chose to set goals at intervals that were not too stressful based on my daily responsibilities. One of the central features of my plan was to memorize one of the seven long surahs every Ramadan.

I started in Ramadan 2015 with surah Al-Baqarah, but I surprised myself by completing the seventh longest surah five years later, just after Ramadan in 2020. During this period, my father went to Umrah in 2017, and when he came home, he suddenly got sick and passed away quickly on July 27 of that same year, which did not allow me the time to go back to Morocco. For the second time since my cousin passed away, I found that focusing on memorization of the Qur'an enabled me to cope with the grieving process. Indeed:

The Qur'an absorbs sadness and grief from the heart like a sponge. If you read the Qur'an while sorrowful and disheartened, it will bandage you, and if you read it while joyful and delighted, it will multiply your happiness. — Dr. Ahmed Aisah Al-Musrawi.

It was well known to the whole family that my father, may Allah (SWT) have mercy on him, was above average in spending time with the Qur'an. He was my role model, and he inspired me to carry on the family tradition and pursue this journey. Therefore, I became reenergized to achieve my goal of memorizing the whole Qur'an.

One thing about my father was that he would never miss a prayer and he would make it on time. For example whenever we were driving on the highway he would always ask us to pull into the next gas station so he could make his prayer, even if we tried to convince him to wait until we arrived at our destination. There is a famous story about him when he was working in France. We have been told that he made prayer regularly at work until his boss found out and told him it is time for work and not for prayer. My father not only left that job but he left France and returned to live in Morocco. Whenever he was asked why he left France he would say, a country in which I cannot make my prayer on time there is no need for me to live in it.

After he returned to Morocco he opened two shops and I remember some time later he went to umrah for three months from Ramadan to Hajj time. During that time even at my young age in secondary school I offered to look after one of the shops, me and my brother Noureddine, although I did miss some school classes during that period. But it was a very good experience to learn how to become responsible and balance between school and business.

28

This is a picture chart of some of the Moroccan freedom fighters referred to as the Flags of the Resistance. I am proud that my Father, second from the left in the bottom row is recognized there. His various responsibilities never stopped him from learning the Qur'an. Sometimes performing the function of an Imam and also operating a business consisting of two shops and raising a family of 17 children did not prevent him from remaining consistent with the Qur'an.

Souad Brown Mhani

Thank you, Allah (SWT), for enabling me to benefit from what I have lost, as it enabled me to be closer and closer to you.

CHAPTER FIVE

I encourage everyone seeking to memorize the Qur'an to list the names of all the surahs, print it out, put it in a conspicuous place like your refrigerator door or next to your bed, and then color the name upon completing memorization of that surah. This will encourage you to maintain your momentum.

Another tip is to memorize the surahs in the order that they appear in the Qur'an. In addition to that, you could memorize one of the seven long surahs during each Ramadan. This suggestion may be suitable for ladies with children who have limited free time and a busy schedule. Most people know that the best time to study is early morning and the latter part of the evening. For those with young children, the best time for memorization would be after their bedtime and before they rise in the morning. For those who have children spread over a number of age brackets, I used to put my youngest child to bed at their appropriate time and then spend some time with my older children, helping them to memorize, which at the same time enabled me to progress with my own memorization. However, for students and people with more free time, I encourage you to follow a more rigorous schedule and take advantage of your period of fewer responsibilities that will increase as you get older.

This chart was my encouragement strategy as it made me consistent. Whenever I completed a surah I would colour it and reward myself. Be consistent do not give up, have a positive and healthy approach toward completion of the surah and recite your daily portion no matter what... you may have to force yourself sometimes and that is the only way. Remember when Allah (SWT) told Prophet John... "Oh Yahya! take hold of the book with strength..." (surah 19:12)

I have a special message for teenagers. Many of my students are teenagers, and I have found that spending time with the Qur'an helps them with their regular schoolwork. I am sure music teachers recognize the similarity in memorizing the Qur'an or learning languages, and children who take such lessons activate the other side of their brains. Memorizing the Qur'an will help you absorb the diverse information that the average high school student has to process on a daily basis. I am confident that if a survey was conducted on teenagers who are at the top of the Qur'an memorization class, you will find that they also achieve good grades in high school.

Believe it or not, many music teachers in Western countries are impressed with the capacity of children to memorize large portions of the Qur'an (i.e., sounds of the words of the Qur'an recited). Many of you may have seen the BBC show about the world Tajweed championship held annually in Cairo. The TV show went to several countries months before the competition to follow the child contestants from all over the Muslim world, including Africa, Asia, the South Pacific, and the Middle East. A Western music teacher was interviewed by the BBC, and she confirmed that the similar positive development of the brain, that studying music causes, is also caused by attending classes on memorizing the Qur'an.

Souad Brown Mhani

Speaking of languages, I learned several languages growing up, Berber from my Father, colloquial Arabic from my mother, classical Arabic and French in primary school, given Morocco's history of being a French colony as French is the second language and it is obligatory to learn it every day. Then later I studied Portuguese, Italian, and Hebrew, in that order. This history in languages was helpful when I turned my attention to memorizing the Qur'an.

Know that music programs in school help your children use parts of the brain that their academic learning may not use to the same extent. Hence, taking music lessons helps develop the other parts of the brain the children can use in their general studies. Therefore, I would like to see a day when all schools that have a sufficient body of interested students offer parents the choice of a music class, languages, a Qur'an memorization class—or all.

When you embark on your quest to memorize the whole Qur'an, it will greatly assist you to team up with one of your friends who shares the same goal. That way you can encourage each other step by step. In my case, one of my cousins, who was my study partner, and I were about to take a test on the first surah we memorized with the online teacher, but neither of us did that well. After that, we decided to help one another by testing each other's memorization ahead of each test. She would recite for me, and then I would recite back to her. This became our regular practice. We referred to each other as our "companion in the Qur'an."

34

It was said choose your friends wisely for indeed you are choosing the front row of your janaza (the funeral prayer).

I feel blessed to be among the people of the Qur'an, and special thanks to my Qur'an companion Rashida.

"The Messenger of Allah said: "Verily Allah has His own people among mankind." They said: O Messenger of Allah, who are they? He said: " They are the people of the Qur'an, Allah's own people and those who are closest to Him."

Here are some additional tips on memorizing the Qur'an:

- Make sure you are clear in your own mind that you are pursuing memorization of the Qur'an to bring yourself closer to Allah (SWT) and that everything else is a secondary benefit. Allah (SWT) said in surah Al-Furqan 25:32: "Thus, that We may strengthen your heart by it."

- Visualization of your success is known to be a strong motivational influence towards achieving the success you have pictured in your mind. In this case, we are talking about visualizing yourself succeeding in reaching your goal of memorization of the Qur'an.

- I find that mornings are the best time for me to memorize. However, each person needs to work out the time that you feel your mind is at its most receptive.

- Most students have found that placing the Qur'an on your left side aids memorization, and the recitation should be in a melody format, applying the rules like *ghunnah*, which is a sound that comes out of the nasal passage that beautifies the recitation. Allah (SWT) said in His book: "And recite the Qur'an with measured recitation." (Al-Muzzammil 73:4)

Many people find it difficult to memorize because they use several Qur'ans. One day they use a Qur'an with a large font, then the next day one with a small font. Or one day a Qur'an with blue paper and then one with white paper. In my experience, I have found that it is much easier to use a Qur'an that has print large enough to read easily, but the book should be a size that can be comfortably with you in your daily activities, and it should be printed on white or light-colored paper so that you can see the smallest markings of Tajweed rules.

Once you choose the Qur'an you want to use for your memorization, do not change it. Use the same Qur'an for however many years needed, and always keep it with you. What I have found is that eventually you can picture in your mind the layout of each page, the first word and last word on each page. This helps you in your memorization, especially if you memorize a page at a time.

As you work your way through each ayah, use a pencil to underline or circle the letters that involve a special Tajweed rule so that you remember the uncommon rules, especially those rules that you find in only one or two places in the Qur'an. For instance, in surah Yussef in ayah 11, where you apply the *Rawm* or *Ishmaam* in the word *ta'manna*; or in surah Hud in ayah 41, where you apply the rule of *Al-Imalah* in the word *majraha* in the letter *R*; or even in surah Fussilat ayah 44, where you apply the rule of *At-Tasehil* (means ease of pronunciation) in the word *A'ajamie*, or the rule of the seven alifaat. In most Qur'ans, you will see uncommon symbols like a diamond shape or a large black or red dot. It depends on the version of your Qur'an.

Also, make sure you don't forget to take your Qur'an with you when you travel. I took mine with me everywhere I traveled, on boats, planes, and trains, and I took advantage of every free minute to revise and memorize. I remember when I traveled from Riyadh to Makkah February 2019, I didn't sleep that much, so I took the opportunity to do memorization. A special memory that is close to my heart is when I was in the bus and I was memorizing ayah 13 in surah Al-Ahzab that talks about the people of Madinah, and I thought to myself that I was on my way to Madinah after I finished my Umrah. After I returned home, I was revising that particular part of the surah, and I got very emotional when I got to that particular ayah that talks about the people of Madinah, because it reminded me of where I was when I started memorizing it.

On another occasion, I took a ferry from the town of Holyhead in the UK to Dublin, and I used the three-and-a-half-hour voyage to do some memorization. I found it very interesting that during the voyage I was memorizing surah Hud, and when I reached ayahs 36-49 that talk about the story of Noah and the ark, I found it symbolic that I was memorizing it while I was on a boat. I would say that by taking your Qur'an with you wherever you go and memorizing it whenever you get a chance will connect memories and encourage you to continue with your memorization.

Concerning the momentum of your memorization, try to add a few new ayats on a regular basis so that your memorization keeps moving through the particular surah. A mistake that many people make is to stay on the same spot too long, thinking they will memorize those few ayahs better, but in fact this approach weakens your memorization. This was recommended by several of my teachers, to revise the old and at the same time memorize the new as you progress. Another technique is to read tomorrow's memorization the night before you go to sleep, because it's known that the last thing you read or see before you go to sleep is easier to remember.

For those occasions when you find yourself having difficulties memorizing certain ayats or surahs, write them down, ideally two or three times, and you will find this will help you to memorize it; most educators will tell you that some people are more visual learners and need to see what they are learning. There is a connection between our handwriting and our mind. What you write comes from the mind, so in fact your brain is seeing the same information several times by you writing the texts rather than just reading them. Many people know that in the early days of Islam, many people used this method in their memorization of the Qur'an. They would not only read the words, but they also wrote them down on wooden writing pads. My father had a similar wooden writing pad that people used many generations ago, and I keep it as a memento.

Souad Brown Mhani

This wooden Qur'anic teaching tablet belonged to my father. He used the traditional method of memorization of Qur'an by writing with a fountain pen dipped in ink or a cut–off feather dip-pen (a quill) dipped in ink. The wooden tablet could be washed off and reused.

As with any project, you should map out your approach to the memorization, the weekly schedule, the time of day or night, and the length of each memorization session. It might be better in the early stages to have short sessions several times a week rather than long sessions. How many months and years you will need will depend on your daily routine.

In my case, I used to memorize daily, and very seldom did I miss a day, because I chose a time of day that I knew would be the quietest for me. For you, it might be mornings, midday, or afternoons. I encourage you to select a realistic, appropriate time that suits you to make it more likely that you will maintain your schedule. It is better to memorize smaller portions of text at regular intervals rather than trying to memorize a large batch frequently. Do you know that some sources indicate that Umar Ibn Al-Khattab (may Allah (SWT) be pleased with him) spent ten years in memorizing surah Al-Baqarah only? It is believed that the *sahabah* (companions of the prophet) used to memorize up to five ayats at a time, and then only after having lived those verses did they move on.

Sticking to your schedule is made easier by choosing a good memorization partner or partners. Today, this is easier because of the internet. Your partner can be anywhere in the world, and you can memorize together for free over any of the numerous voice over internet (VOI) applications.

41

It is good if you have at least one memorization partner. The great benefit from learning with good partners is that it generates a natural competitive spirit. When I found out that some of my closest friends that started this journey with me had already finished the Qur'an or had progressed ahead of me, it inspired my competitive energy and drove me forward. I thank my friends for helping me and inspiring the drive to finish.

My Qur'an memorization partner is related to me, my cousin Rachida. She lives in a time zone only one hour ahead of mine. She lives in the south of France, and I live in the UK. I have to say that my task was made easier because of the participation of my cousins, particularly Rachida, and Hasana, because they helped to lighten the load. There were times when we used to be in the middle of an ayah and stopped to discuss the feelings we got from it. Then there were other times when we were so tired and started pronouncing the words incorrectly or mixing the surah with another that we just took an unscheduled break and had a lighthearted chat.

Even better, if there is an Islamic studies school in your area, you should attend their Qur'an memorization classes. This will help to reenforce the accuracy of your pronunciation and your focus on learning the articulation points of the letters, and then the characteristics of the letters, which are what differentiate letters from others that share the same articulation point. For example, the letters *kaf* and *qaf* have the same articulation point, but the characteristic of the letter *qaf* is heavy, while the letter *kaf* is light. Applying the wrong sound may incorrectly refer to a different word.

"Allah has sent down the best statement: a consistent Book wherein is reiteration." (Qur'an 39:23)

There are numerous online tools to assist a student in memorizing the Qur'an. One of my favorites is Sheikh Ayman Suwayd. I benefited a lot from this online resource.

The Prophet PBUH said, "The best among you (Muslims) are those who learn Qur'an and teach it." (Sahib Al-Bukhari 5027, Book 66, Hadith 49, Vol. 6, Book 61, Hadith 545)

From what I have been taught about this hadith by my Qira'at sheikhah, it does not mean that you should take away from studying towards your chosen profession, rather, that you should set aside part of your free time to devote to memorizing the Qur'an. For example, you can get up thirty minutes or an hour earlier and devote that time. Or go to bed thirty minutes or one hour later to devote that time to studying, and you will receive the blessings spoken about in the hadith.

Further evidence to emphasize the associated benefits of devoting the time to studying is found in the following verses:

Oh mankind, there has to come to you instruction from your Lord and healing for what is in the breasts and guidance and mercy for the believers. (Qur'an 10:57)

And We send down of the Qur'an that which is healing and mercy for the believers. (Qur'an 17:82)

The following ayat also adequately reinforced my point: "The Most Merciful, taught the Qur'an." (Surah Ar-Rahman 55:01-02) I refer specifically to the word *Ar-Rahman,* which conveys that the acquiring of this knowledge is a mercy.

The next step is to learn the Tajweed rules and try to apply them. I find that although a person can memorize to pronounce a word correctly, it is better to know why you pronounce certain letters the way that you do. If there is no madrassah in your area, there are numerous very qualified Qur'an memorization teachers online. The reason why I have recommended you have a qualified teacher in addition to your memorization partners is because you must not guess at applying the

Tajweed rules, especially because you want to properly understand the symbols you will come across in several spots in the Qur'an that point to special rules of Tajweed. The hardest thing to do is to correct your memory after you have memorized something incorrectly.

My advice, especially for teenagers and young people who are attending university, is to seek friends who regularly attend the masjid (mosque). I am not talking about memorization partners. I am referring to regular friends, because if your regular friends practice their religion, they will be inclined to encourage you to keep to your memorization schedule once they learn of your goals. This is something I have done whenever I have moved my residence. I always found a local masjid and befriended people who were already involved in learning the Qur'an.

In my case, because of my preexisting qualifications in Tajweed rules and my love for teaching the Qur'an, when I moved to London in September 2018, I wanted my children to attend a madrassah, because I didn't want them to forget what I taught them when I had homeschooled them the year before. After doing research, I was recommended to contact the administrator of the Al Barakah School, which I was told had a remarkably high standard of teaching. By the bounty of Allah (SWT), I started teaching there and also registered my children as students. My children have learned a lot, and they look forward to attending the school every weekend. I would like to use this opportunity to thank the administration, my lovely students, and the Al Barakah community for the high-quality institution they have created.

My advice for approaching memorization is similar to how you would approach any investment. When you invest or start a business, you have an initial float that you leave in the business or investment; that is your foundation. As you make a profit, you take those profits and leave the float to support your continuing investment activity. You do not want to take a loss, because the loss of money will reduce your float and weaken your ongoing business activity. Investing in memorizing the Qur'an is similar, because you determine what you want to be the foundation of your memorization, and then you focus on retaining that while at the same time adding newly memorized surahs. You can use the first *Juzaa* (a part of the Qu'ran) that you learned as your memorization float or foundation, and no matter what surah you are memorizing at a given time, you ensure that you retain full memory of that first Juzaa. If you do not do this, you risk losing the memorization of your foundation in the Qur'an, which may discourage you from continuing.

Another thing to remember is to pick an occasion, whether it is one month or whatever interval you find works best for you, to recite everything you have memorized up to that point, even if you have to look at the text to help you in parts where your memory may be weak. Repetitive memorization is more important than *hifdh (memorization)*, because it will entrench the Qur'an into the seat of your subconscious, that part of you that remains to the end on a person's deathbed.

One thing I have found very helpful in this modern era of technological gadgets and devices like sophisticated mobile phones is that it is easy for you to record your recitation and then play it back while at the same time looking at the text to check the quality of your recitation. You could record into your computer or other device, but I prefer to use my phone because it's smaller and easier to carry and listen to when I get a chance.

TECHNIQUE FOR MEMORIZATION OR REVISION

This chart is based on Surah An-Naba (78) as a current memorization target shown in the second column. The fourth column sets out how to prepare for the next memorization target Surah (77)

Days	Surah 78 An-Naba	Recite in Sunnah prayer	target Surah (77) Al-Mursalat
Monday	From ayah 1 to 7	****	Read 3 times
Tuesday	From ayah 8-14	From ayah 1 to 7	Read 3 times
Wednesday	From ayah 15-21	From ayah 8-14	Read 3 times
Thursday	From ayah 22-29	From ayah 15-21	Read 3 times
Friday	From ayah 30-37	From ayah 22-29	Read 3 times
Saturday	From ayah 38-40	From ayah 30-37	Read 3 times
Sunday	From ayah 1-40	From ayah 38-40	Read 3 times

If you preserve the Qur'an in your memory it will preserve you. Therefore, it isn't about how far you've reached in Qur'an, but also about how far it has reach in you.

I remember when I first started memorizing, it took me a long time to complete even one page, sometimes up to one hour or more. However, after the first few months, my ability to remember strengthened, and my memorization of a page of the Qur'an began to take less than half the time compared to when I first started on this unforgettable journey. I used to memorize one long surah each Ramadan, but once I reached the twentieth Juzaa, I realized the end of my task was in sight and, like a runner on their final lap in the race, I accelerated to ensure I passed the finish line in the best manner possible.

You will receive special rewards on your journey to memorize the Qur'an. They will be cherished memories highlighted by special occasions, as if you had your private and personal memory at your various surah memorization points.

One of my most memorable surah locations is when my Qur'an partner, my cousin Rachida, and I were discussing what surah we should memorize next, because we usually memorized in order from surah Al-Kahf going towards the front of the Qur'an. Then we memorized from the surah before Al Kahf towards the other part.

My cousin and I continued memorizing until we reached to surah Al-Anfal. On this occasion, it was getting near to Ramadan. We were supposed to move on to the next surah, which is surah Al-A'raf, but when I took a quick look at how many ayahs it has, I noticed it has more ayahs than the surah after it. So I suggested to my cousin that we should start with the shorter surah Al-An'am and leave the longer one for Ramadan because I knew I would have more free time to tackle the task. Some days went by until we agreed to skip the next surah and memorize the shorter one.

After we finished memorizing the shorter surah, we did indeed tackle the longer surah during Ramadan as it was during the Covid-19 lockdown in our respective countries and we used to memorize one page in the time after taraweeh and until Suhur (predawn meal). I only realized towards the end of surah Al-A'raf, which we reached after the end of Ramadan, that it ends with a *sajdah* (prostration). Completing Ramadan while at the same time completing the memorization of the surah just after the end of Ramadan was a special memory for me, especially doing so with a sajdah.

I felt like I was blessed with four Eids in one. Eid
Al-Fitr felt kind of special, giving that it was during the
pandemic and that all the masjids had been closed. And
because people were not going to work, I was able to do
Ramadan with the whole family present. The second of
the four Eids was that the UK phases of returning back
to normal were starting just after Eid Al-Fitr. The third
of the four Eids was my birthday because it occurred
just after Eid, although as Muslims we do not celebrate
our birthdays. I felt like I was reborn when I completed
the Qur'an, and the fourth Eid was my finishing the
memorization of the Qur'an, especially with the sajdah
that was not planned. So, this special memory is that it
was planned by Allah (SWT) as it just happened, so I
understood it to be one of the many gifts that you receive
during this blessed journey. So, surah Al A'raf has joined
the selection of my favorite surahs.

When it comes to memorizing the Qur'an, it may look
like an impossible task to some people, but you have to
make your pure intention to Allah (SWT) first and renew
that intention on a regular basis. Furthermore, take your time
in choosing your Qur'an partner, because they can either
make you stronger or weaker. Remember to select a Qur'an
with clear print, ideally thin print, not thick. Make lots of
duas, and ask Allah (SWT) to fixate your heart on wanting

to complete the memorization and to make Qur'an your best and constant companion in this world and the next. Keep company with like-minded students of the Qur'an at least once a week and try your best to revise what you learned that week and the previous week. Another useful tip is to read the Qur'an daily, even if only for half an hour. When you reach difficulty in keeping to your memorization schedule, make adjustments that enable you to continue until you find the right system that works for you.

One of the mistakes many people make is that they move on to the next surah without trying to connect the verses they have been memorizing in segments. So, on completing a surah, before you move on to the next one, you should be able to recite it from memory from beginning to end. If you recite all your newly memorized surahs in all your sunnah salahs, it will improve your memorization and focus during prayer. The newly memorized surahs will take more of your concentration to ensure your pronunciation and applying the Tajweed rules are correct, which as you know is important during the salah (prayer).

HOW LONG DOES IT TAKE TO MEMORIZE THE QUR'AN?

Abd-Allaah ibn 'Amr narrated that the Prophet (peace and blessings of Allaah be upon him) said:

"It will be said to the companion of the Qur'an: 'Recite and rise in status as you used to recite in the world, and your position will be at the last verse you recite.'"

Daily Amount	Time to Completion
1 verse	17 years, 7 months, 9 days
2 verses	8 years, 9 months, 18 days
3 verses	5 years, 10 months, 13 days
4 verses	4 years, 4 months, 24 days
5 verses	3 years, 6 months, 7 days
6 verses	2 years, 11 months, 4 days
7 verses	2 years, 6 months, 3 days
8 verses	2 years, 2 months, 12 days
9 verses	1 year, 11 months, 12 days
10 verses	1 year, 9 months, 3 days
11 verses	1 year, 7 months, 6 days
12 verses	1 year, 5 months, 15 days
13 verses	1 year, 4 months, 6 days
14 verses	1 year, 3 months
15 verses	1 year, 2 months, 1 day
16 verses	1 year, 1 month, 6 days
17 verses	1 year, 10 days
18 verses	11 months, 19 days
19 verses	11 months, 1 days
Half page	3 years, 4 months, 21 days
One page	1 year, 8 months, 12 days
Two Pages	10 months, 6 days

Another thing I want to leave you with is that when you are reciting the Qur'an, ask yourself what is it that Allah (SWT) wants to teach you through this ayah. Also, when you read an ayah that's talking about a story of a prophet, contemplate what lesson Allah (SWT) wants you to learn from that story. Additionally, coming across an ayah while reciting that says, "O You who believe," or "O Mankind," it means that Allah (SWT) is talking to you and has a message for you.

Do they not then reflect on the Qur'an? Or are there locks upon their hearts? (Qur'an 47:24)

This is a blessed Book which We have revealed to you O prophet so that they may contemplate its verses, and people of reason may be mindful. (Qur'an 38:29)

Therefore, if you come across an ayah about paradise or hellfire, pause and reflect at those times so that you seek the message for you, and always make a dua that you will be among the people of paradise when the ayah talks about paradise and seek refuge when it talks about hellfire.

In my case, I always reflect when I read the following ayah in surah An-Nisaa: "Wavering between them, [belonging] neither to the believers nor to the disbelievers. And whoever Allah leaves astray, never will you find for him a way." (Qur'an 4:143)

And one more of my favorite ayats in the Qur'an is in surah At-Tur, where Allah (SWT) says: "Therefore, wait for the judgement of your Rabb with patience, We are surely watching over you. Glorify your Rabb with His praises when you wake up." (Qur'an 52:48)

Set yourself the goal of reading the complete Qur'an (not necessarily from memory) once a month or once every two months, depending on your best efforts. This continuous rereading has many benefits, such as improving your familiarity of words that are repeated so many times in the Qur'an, which will help you to identify the surahs in which they appear and will help you picture the structure of the surahs and the ayats in your mind. You will find that by maintaining your memorization schedule, your vocabulary will improve, as will your knowledge of tafseer, your pronunciation, and the fluency of your reading. Translate key words into your own language on a regular basis, because it is so important that you understand the central message in each portion of the Qur'an that you memorize. The building of your Arabic vocabulary will definitely help you to be able to segregate the Qur'an to fit your daily experience and recall relevant ayats to any points you discuss with friends and relatives. Just like you know the days of the week and the months of the year, this exercise will imprint in your memory the names of all the surahs and the order in which they appear.

CHAPTER SIX

You will never forget the day on which you finish memorizing the Qur'an. For me, I remember very clearly it was on a Friday. My Qur'an partner Rachida was very enthusiastic, encouraging me to complete the last ten ayah that were left for us to memorize, but I kept delaying, trying to find a more convenient time. So, I finished on Friday, June 5, 2020, when Rachida called me to memorize the last surah together. When we reached the last ayah, and after we practiced reading it many times, she recited it without looking. Then it was my turn. I told her I could do it by myself, but at that particular moment she received a phone call and put me on hold. I waited for a few seconds, then I kept practicing the last ayah, and I recited it out loud to myself. That last ayah, as I mentioned before, ends with a prostration, so I did the sajdah, and I remembered my father and made lots of duas for him with many tears of mixed emotions. All of a sudden I heard my cousin back on the phone, so I told her that her phone call came at a good time because it enabled me to have personal reflections as I completed the memorization.

"Say, 'All this (revelation of the Qur'an) is through the grace of Allah and His mercy. In this, therefore, let them rejoice, (because) this (Qur'an) is better than all that they hoard." Qur'an 10:58.

Memorization of the Qur'an is a gift from Allah (SWT), not an achievement of your intellect, even though many may assume so. Proof of this is that people memorize the Qur'an at different rates, some fast, some slow. Those with a high IQ may find it more difficult to memorize than so-called educational underachievers. Therefore I am appreciative and make duas of thanks to Allah (SWT) for granting me a path that made it easy to memorize the Qur'an.

It is known that memorization is divided into four types:

1. You may memorize quickly but forget quickly. The way to overcome this is to revise daily.

2. You are the type of person who may memorize quickly but also retain longer (i.e., forget slowly). This is one of Allah's (SWT) mercies that you should take advantage of.

3. You are the type of person who memorizes very slowly but then forgets quickly. The treatment for this is to leave sinful behavior behind, increase your good deeds, and revise daily.

4. You are the type of person who memorizes very slowly but then forgets very slowly. This is a reward from Allah (SWT) for your persistence when memorization does not come easy for you.

I recall this surah that may be relevant: "We have not revealed the Quran to you 'O Prophet' to cause you distress." (Qur'an 20:02). You must have a state of mind that the effort to memorize the Qur'an is not a burden. Set a pace that you can manage that still makes it an enjoyable experience. If you do that, you will look forward to the sessions you set aside for memorization.

From my experience, if you place consistency as one of your priorities, memorizing the Qur'an will be made easier for you. Allah (SWT) said in His Holy Book: "For it is truly a mighty Book." (Qur'an 41:41)

A good example is if you place the consistency of your salah as one of your priorities, it becomes quickly established in your daily activity with ease. For example, whether you are in a wedding party or some other entertainment event, you remain uncomfortable when the time for salah passes and you need to find an appropriate place in the vicinity to make your prayers and then return to the event that you are attending. This is the benefit that derives from placing learning the Qur'an and making the prayer at a high level among your priorities.

"You do not guide whom you like, but Allah guides whom He wills." (Qur'an 28:56)

This memorization became a part of my daily routine, the most important part. I took every single opportunity to memorize: when cooking my favorite dishes, while cleaning my messy kitchen, while in waiting rooms for an appointment, while dropping and picking up the kids from school, as well as when resting my exhausted body from a long, busy day. During this special journey, an appropriate ayah that came to my mind is: "As for those who struggle in Our cause, We will surely guide them along Our way." (Qur'an 29:69)

I came to the realization from a single experience that the right time will never come unless you strive for it and have relied on the might and power of Allah (SWT). The benefits of memorizing the Qur'an are too numerous to mention, but some of the well-known benefits are conveyed by scholars. Imagine yourself on your first night in the grave—no relatives, father, mother, or siblings. You are lonely, and all of a sudden the Qur'an that you memorized with lots of effort and time provides proof that it was a sound investment, because you realize it is a bright light illuminating your grave, and it turns it into a garden—the gardens of paradise. And let's not forget about the hadith of the Prophet, peace and blessings be upon him, who said: "It will be said to the companion of the Qur'an: recite and ascend as you recited in the world. Verily, your rank is determined by the last verse you recite." (Sunan al-Tirmidhi 2914)

Another benefit explained in a hadith that the Prophet (PBUH) said: "Whoever reads the Qur'an, learns it, and acts in accordance with it, on the day of resurrection, his parents will be given a crown to wear whose light be like the light of the sun, and his parents will be given garments which far surpass everything that is found in this world. They will say, 'Why have we been given this to wear?' It will be said, 'Because your child learned the Qur'an.'" (Al-Haakim; Al-Albani: authentic, on Saheeh At-Targheeb).

Know that time passes quickly, so *be careful* to spend it wisely, and do not be distracted by the never-ending tests we all experience. Also, remember that putting the Qur'an into practice will straighten your soul and purify your heart, so if you memorize surah Al Ma'un that says, "So woe to those 'hypocrites' who pray," you should adopt and implement the message.

> *[This is] a blessed Book which We have revealed to you, [O Muhammad], that they might reflect upon its verses and those of understanding would be reminded. (Qur'an 38:29)*

Memorizing the Qur'an is a big *amanah* and responsibility, as its benefits are real, particularly to reflecting your character and your manners, so our *deen* (religion) is upon our *akhlaq* (manners).

"Qatadah reported: 'I said to Aisha, 'O mother of the believers, tell me about the character of the messenger of Allah, peace and blessings be upon him.' Aisha said,

'Have you not read the Qur'an?' I said, 'Of course.' Aisah said, 'Verily, the character of the prophet of Allah was the Qur'an.'" (Sahih Muslim 746 Grade: Sahih (authentic) according Muslim)

I now have a better understanding and deeper perspective of the following ayah: "Do people think once they say, 'We believe,' that they be left without being put to the test?" (Qur'an 29:1)

It is said that if you look carefully enough at even what are considered to be bad occurrences, there will be some benefits in them. The world went into lockdown in February 2020 because of the COVID-19 pandemic, shutting down all the airports, cancelling flights, closing schools. Most jobs were closed, with the majority of the population in every country forced to stay at home for months. I even had to homeschool my children because their school closed. I had more time to spend on memorization because I didn't have to go to work every day. Therefore, a benefit from the COVID-19 pandemic is that it enabled me to finish ahead of schedule. I am sure all readers who witnessed the period of the pandemic in the first half of 2020 remember how tranquil and quiet society became, and it was the best time to engage in memorization of the Qur'an because of the reduction in distractions and a more natural home life.

My journey to memorize the Qur'an took six years. Your journey may take less or more, but the important thing is that during the process you take the time to reflect on what you want to internalize from the experience. It seemed like my six-year journey passed faster than the four years I spent at university. This is why it is important that you pause at regular intervals to reassess your main goal. For me, completing the memorization of the Qur'an made me feel that I had added to my educational accomplishments, and we all know the well-known saying: "Seek knowledge from the cradle to the grave." Therefore, after you finish the task of memorization, as I said earlier, you can go through the Qur'an a second time, or you can pick any other field of Islamic studies to expand your knowledge in your religion. One of my wishes is that at least one of my children develops a similar desire to memorize the whole of the Qur'an in sha Allah.

With respect to what I wish my readers receive from this first and special book, initially I was under an inspiring illusion that before anyone can embark on memorizing the Qur'an or undertake a project like writing this book that they have to have complete peace and quietness of mind. I believed I would have to wait to start memorization until I had the right time. The perfect conditions I was looking for was when my mind was clear, like walking through the park early in the morning when the air is fresh and there were no people to disturb my thoughts; when my daily regimen balanced, such as regular sleep patterns, regular eating times, regular work hours, etc., or when all the things I believe were my priorities were either completed or under control. I envisioned I would have to be free from all responsibilities of daily life in order to start memorization of the Qur'an.

Eventually, I realized that memorization should be achievable by an ordinary person if it's true that memorization of the Qur'an is naturally possible. It should not be possible only for persons who locked themselves away from society, became full-time professional students, or had to somehow become a nonfunctioning, regular person. If that were the case, no one would aspire to complete the task. Therefore, I undertook this journey as a regular person dealing with everyday problems and responsibilities of daily life as a working mother of four school-age children.

I am now on my second *khatmah* (completing the memorization of the entire Qur'an), paying more detailed attention under the guidance of an expert sheikhah who was one of my earlier, strict teachers who had left to start her own private classes, and I am pleased she is teaching me again. Now that I know the surahs from my first memorization, we are focusing on very precise rules at the expert level. Therefore, do not consider that your journey is over, because although you have completed your goal, now you need to perfect it. What you will find if you do that is that your friends and relatives will come to you for advice and answers in their own interactions with the Qur'an. You will want to have the confidence to know that you are giving them sound and correct advice. So, really, your first khatmah is about laying the foundation for your deeper study of the Qur'an.

Once you finish your memorization objective, you will want to use that free time to build on your Islamic knowledge. "Seeking knowledge is an obligation upon every Muslim." (Source: Ibn Majah 224) You will recall the difficulties and pressures that you experienced along the way and how much of a relief the feeling of having a much lighter load felt. But do not fill this new free time you will experience for frivolous activities, use it to expand other aspects of your Islamic knowledge. "Are those who know equal with those who do not know? But only men of understanding will pay heed." [39:9]. I have signed up for classes for Qira'at and am finding it wonderfully interesting and complementary to my Qur'anic studies, and I hope one day to write a book about that fascinating subject!

Review Requested:
We'd like to know if you enjoyed the book. Please consider leaving a review on the platform from which you purchased the book.

Lightning Source UK Ltd.
Milton Keynes UK
UKHW022302010621
384764UK00006B/108